THE PERMISSION

HOW TO GIVE IT, TAKE IT, OR NOT NEED IT AT ALL

JESSICA M. REESE

THE PERMISSION: HOW TO GIVE IT, TAKE IT, OR NOT NEED IT AT ALL

Copyright © 2022 Jessica Reese

Published by Ink to Legacy Publishing

Blythewood, South Carolina 29016

www.ink2legacy.com

978-1-7363674-6-9 (pbk)

978-1-7363674-7-6 (ebook)

Printed in the United States of America

The Permission

Permission is defined as consent or authorization. If you dissect the word permission into two parts – *per* and *mission*, per means each and mission means an important assignment. Life is filled with important assignments that only you have been designed to complete. As you continue to travel down the road called life, you will find yourself seeking permission from others to do, say, go, and have based on your needs, wants and desires.

As you continue to live and embark on each assignment for your life, take a pause and evaluate where you should grant yourself permission to fulfill what you need, want and desire.

This book was written with you in mind, yes YOU...

-The Dreamer, who dreams big, but because you have not seen anyone else do it, being the first is frightening

-The Responsible One, who lives by the blueprint created by others, yet you were never considered in the design

-The Loyal One, who is everyone else's rock, confidant, and sounding board, yet no one asks how you are doing or what you need

-The Life of the Party, who always pours from your cup, yet no one offers to fill yours

-The Great Friend, who shows up for everyone else, yet you don't show up for yourself

-The Trailblazer, who thinks outside of the box, yet you are controlled by other people's fears

-The Entrepreneur, who hears the applause from strangers, yet the silence from your family and friends is deafening at times

-The Wife, who submitted to her husband and his plans, yet you too want to see your plans come into fruition

-The Mother, who tells her child they can be and do anything they to be, yet refuses to live their dreams out loud

-The Child, who is their parent's pride and joy, yet seldom felt celebrated or seen

-The Person, who wants to take off the mask and be your authentic self, yet you have never seen yourself without it

Do Yourself a Favor...Take a Deep Breath and Prepare to Give Yourself Permission

If you are honest with yourself, the life you are living is built on permission...not permission from others, but the permission you continuously give to yourself or not.

As you read about my journey and how I had to learn to give myself permission if I was ever going to live a life of purpose on purpose, you will quickly discover that choices had to be made, decisions had to be honored and boundaries had to be enforced, to become the best version of myself...Jessica Michelle.

It has been a journey, and will continue to be, because that is the beauty of evolution.

Permission Slips

(Table of Contents)

The Power in Giving Myself Permission

Be honest, do you remember the first time you went outside to play? Your first time eating a piece of candy? Or even the first television show you watched? I am sure after much ponder; the response would be a resounding no...to all three questions. Your response would be no, not because those first experiences were horrible, but because it is difficult to remember experiences where you did not have a say in the who, what, when where or how.

Just like my first time playing outside, tasting chocolate candy and the first television program I watched, these and other "firsts" in life were guided by someone deciding on my behalf the options for me to consider, then granting me permission to experience what was being offered.

Life has a funny way of revealing options. I would love to say I knew from childhood I would become an award-winning hairstylist. I would love to say I knew I would become a successful entrepreneur. I would love to say I knew that when I founded The Pynk Butterfly, it would become the beauty brand it is today. I would love to say that I knew, but if I am honest, I cannot. I cannot say I knew; I can only say I had hoped. But I only began to hope when I gave myself permission.

Growing up in Georgia, I had the best of both worlds. Although my parents were divorced, I never felt the tug of war often experienced by children living between two parents. My parents speaking ill of each other or about their family members was a foreign language to me. In fact, I would say I lived in a bubble. I cannot speak for anyone else, but it was all sun, moon, and stars in my neck of the woods. My parents got along. My grandparents got along. My cousins were more like siblings. We were all one big happy family...everybody got along. Even when my mother remarried, I gained a dad, and both of my dads got along. I already shared with you that my parents got divorced and my mom remarried. But what I did not share was that I refer to her wedding as our wedding. Yes, we got married. During the wedding ceremony, after they exchanged vows, my "new dad" picked me up and made a commitment to me too. He not only gained a wife but a daughter. It was my day just as much as it was their day. So, cheers to the three of us, and every year it is Happy Anniversary…to us! I know some people would call it a fairytale; I call it family.

Family, yes family. How does a simple 6-letter word have the power to ignite such a complex wave of emotions? I know when I hear the word family, I am quickly filled with fond memories created by great people. For example, my paternal grandmother Maboo, as she is affectionately known, who loved working with her hands, was known for throwing down in the kitchen and being a seamstress. She knew how to feed you and make you look good. My paternal grandfather, PaPa was a sharecropper and businessman, and you better believe Maboo kept him looking like Georgia's finest. My maternal grandmother was a teacher. I learned from her early in life that education was the one thing no one could take away from you. In fact, my grandmother made sure her children, her children's children, and anyone else she could help, not only pursued higher education but that they felt supported while doing it. To my grandmother, education was the key to unlock opportunity and she made sure everyone who wanted a key, had a key.

My other grandmother, Nannie, was a retired educator who returned to teaching, and was very active in the Presbyterian church. Nannie loved crocheting. When I was 8 years old she gifted me with a blanket that I still sleep with to this day. Against my mother's wishes, it went to college with me. Africa, China, Jamaica, New York, and the list goes on, this blanket has gone everywhere with me and should probably have its own frequent flyer miles account.

Long before discovering the benefits of Triple A, I discovered Triple E. I got to see up front and personal the value of experience, exposure, and education. When I consider the big picture of life, I believe family truly is our first real introduction to the world of opportunity. Afterall, we become what we see. And just like the old saying, "You have to see it to be it," I saw it. On one side of my family, I had an example of what it looked like to leave college after the first year to pursue a passion. I saw what it looked like to work at a Black owned "first of its kind" business in an affluent community. I saw what it looked like to build a life and career based on passion. On the other side of my family, I saw that dedication to higher education looked like relocating your household to another state to complete a doctoral program or earning a bachelor's degree then returning to college to earn a MBA. Whether it was the pursuit of passion or the pursuit of education, the foundation for me to stand on was created with love, support, and a spirit of excellence. The lens for me to view the opportunities this life had to offer was shaped and sharpened by family. I learned early in life that failure was not an option, at least not for me.

But what happens when what you have pursued and worked so hard to obtain, just does not work for you anymore? What happens when the dream position becomes a nightmare? When the lucrative compensation becomes an anchor, keeping you in one place? What happens when the passion you have muffled for so long begins stirring up, making a scene, and disrupting your peace?

I had to ask myself and I will ask you, why don't we pursue what we love? Why don't we pursue what we enjoy? I believe it is because we do not see anyone else doing it. We see everyone else around us following a blueprint that appears to be working because they have all the things that they "want and need," so from the natural eye, it appears that ALL IS WELL. But is it all well? Do they have what they want and need, or do they have what appears to be what they want and need? Society bombards us with timelines, to-do lists, and where are you now questions, which turn into our timelines, our to-do lists and what have I done with my life self-hating and self-sabotaging thoughts and actions.

I mean who told me I could not...I could not pursue, I could not go, I could not try? Guess who? Guess who had the unmitigated gall to tell me I could not...I did! Yes, I did. I told myself. Now, I did not use the exact words – YOU CAN'T, but I did demonstrate what I thought through my actions, or should I say lack of action. What was laid before me, was my path...so I trained myself to think.

Who was I to think that I could play twister with my life?

9

Twister...you remember the game Twister, where you step on one colored circle, then extend your leg to another colored circle, which happened to be quite a distance away, which caused you to stretch beyond what was comfortable, only to be told to balance yourself and do not fall. Do not fall...how was I not to fall with one leg here, one leg there, one arm over there and the other arm way over there, all while trying to keep the weighted pressures of life off the person who came behind me, under me. If I fell, they would be crushed. If I did not hold it together, they would not have a chance. "If I did not," was the undeserved pressure that I constantly found myself and others find themselves carrying. Enough is enough. If I were truly going to live life on my terms and live a life that I could be proud of, I was going to have to make some decisions and they all started with giving myself permission.

I
AM A
WELL
KEPT
SECRET!

Permission To Change My Mind

When I stepped foot onto the campus of Spelman College, I knew I had officially become part of a rich legacy that had made its imprint on the community, country, and world. With excitement and ready to become part of that legacy, I knew the next 4 years would be filled with experiences, changes, exploration, and discoveries. Was I ready? Absolutely. Well, at least I thought I was. I quickly discovered something new about myself - I did not know how to study.

Everyone always said studying in college is quite different from studying in high school. Boy, ain't that the truth! In fact, it was completely different. I was declared a Psychology with a Pre-Med concentration major...why I do not know. I did not even want to go into medicine, but like many life decisions I did what I thought was expected, accepted, and the responsible thing to do. In full transparency, becoming a medical professional was not part of my dream. Even as I negotiated with myself to try and stick it out, I was also negotiating with my professors, telling them, "If you let me pass, I promise I won't become a doctor". I know that sounds funny, but there were times that my responses to multiple choice questions were actually short answers. Selecting A, B, C or D - all the above, was not an option for me. In the margins of the exams, I would write full explanations as my responses to questions. I smile now, but I know my professors where thinking, "What in the world?". They probably thought I was being silly, but I called it being scholarly.

Once I committed to my major, the wind beneath my sail was undeniable. Time really did pass by quickly. Before I knew it, it was graduation time. And with graduation quickly approaching, it also meant I was being recruited by companies to launch a potential career. At that time, HBCUs (Historically Black Colleges and Universities) were for a lack of better words, sexy. They were being revered as the place to find high-achieving African American candidates, who were destined for greatness. You know, cream of the crop. Truth be told everybody wanted HBCU graduates on their company roster. It was undeniable. From the Fortune 5 to Fortune

500 companies, securing students from HBCUs was the thing to do.

My final decision came down to two companies – Pfizer and Philip Morris USA – now Altria Group. After much consideration and counsel, I chose Philip Morris USA. Did it help that I was recruited by someone who looked like me? Absolutely. The power of representation was and still is real. It is not just a catch phrase or cliché; it really has the power to change one's perspective. I can recall some of the countless conversations where I weighed the pros and cons of launching my career with either company, but it would be one piece of advice that would seal the deal for me. "Jessica, Philip Morris USA is the training ground for wherever you want to go. They will train you at top dollar to do whatever you will do anywhere else". And boy, they did just that. While I truly did not feel like my course of study married well with Philip Morris USA, the recruiter who looked like me and sounded like my mom, reassured me that my degree represented the most important thing, that I could learn.

As the old saying goes, you do not have to tell me twice. All I could think was look out world, Jessica Michelle has arrived, and I was ready. With my bags packed, I headed to Greenville, South Carolina to launch my career in the real world.

I must have demonstrated my ability to learn quickly because promotion after promotion had my name on it. I was climbing that corporate ladder and was on way to the top. I started off as a territory sales manager in Spartanburg, South Carolina, where sales revenue ranged from 2 to 4 million dollars for the territory. Shortly after I was then promoted to a unit manager in Columbia, South Carolina, where there was one management team with five units in each district. I was the only female. Yes, you read that right, the only female. Just imagine being the only anything, anywhere. Sound fun? Or does it sound like a decision needed to be made. Yes, I could have settled just being a spectator and let decisions about me be made for me by people around me, or I could choose to actively and intentionally participate in my success. Let's just say I chose the latter. Every time I showed up, I was comfortable asking for what I wanted and what I needed. It challenged everything in me from being comfortable. Intimidation did not live here. I channeled my grandmother who always told me to open my mouth, talk, and enunciate my words. And since closed mouths do not get fed or heard, I let my voice be heard. Blame my upbringing, but I did not see mealy-mouth women growing up. They said what they wanted and what they needed without hesitation or stutter.

Armed with confidence, support of a great mentor, who was the woman that recruited me, I treated my unit just like a business. I was responsible for hundreds of stores. They included retail chains, convenience stores and independently owned locations. As you probably have already guessed, management in these stores did not look like me. Imagine the looks of surprise when I arrived at store sites, inviting their management to my negotiation table or when it was my signature required to close the deal. Or how about when my site visits called for me to have the difficult conversations. Having to tell someone they will not receive their monthly compensation, knowing they relied on it to pay for things like company overhead or their child's tuition was never an easy conversation to have. Did I have to give myself pep talks before delivering such news? Yes. Did I recognize for some that me being the messenger was worse than the news itself? Yes. Did that stop me from doing my job? Absolutely not. In fact, I kept that same energy when it was time to have the celebratory conversations too. I had a job to do, and I did it well.

There is no denying my success in Corporate America. I spent 8 years at Philip Morris USA, and the taste of success was sweet. Looking back, it truly was a training ground for how to manage life personally and professionally. From learning and refining my time management and organizational skills to managing multiple objectives and developing a strong business acumen, I was a solider on the field. Was it hard work? Yes. Were the rewards great? Yes. From high compensating salaries and bonuses to expense accounts and company cars, I would emphatically say the rewards were great. But unfortunately, that is what kept me and keeps a lot of people on the field, the rewards or as I like to call them, golden handcuffs.

The pseudo security of shiny golden handcuffs comes with a cost. While they appear to be holding you securely to a corporate ladder, the shiny glare makes you forget to count the costs dangling in our blind spots. The missed dinners, holidays, celebrations, family events, vacations, funerals, or being actively involved in the community are all costs...costs that we fail to count.

It is easy to get comfortable, not just in the lifestyle you live, but in keeping the pause button pressed down on your dreams and goals. That was me. In the back of my mind and deep in my heart I always knew what I wanted to do, but I was comfortable...until I got uncomfortable.

My husband and I decided to start our family. With my diagnosis of Polycystic Ovarian Syndrome (PCOS), conceiving without assistance would be unlikely. Filled with hope, I knew I was going to have a baby. I did not know when, but I knew it would happen. I remember going to the pharmacy to pick up a prescription and the pharmacist telling me it could take a year before I would get pregnant. If say less was a person, she would be the poster child. I knew it was her responsibility to inform me of the facts and potential outcomes of the medication but hearing the words "a year" did deflate some of the air out of my balloon of expectation.

After one month, I found out I was pregnant. We were having a baby. During a routine checkup it was discovered that when I laughed my cervix opened and caused alarm. Without hesitation, the doctor put me on bedrest immediately. He instructed my husband to take me home and informed us I would need to be on bedrest for the duration of my pregnancy. That meant from July to November I would be home, in the bed, all day and all night.

I am convinced that negotiation is in my blood. Do you know I asked the doctor if I could finish out the rest my week at work, then go on bedrest? Yes, you read that right. I was told that my cervix was appearing to slightly open when I laughed, coughed, or any type of pressure was made, which meant my baby was at risk, but I was worried about finishing out the work week. Sad, but true. It was not that I did not care about my health or the health of my baby, it is just that I was committed to completing what I started. I took pride in my work and pulling my weight, but this would be the time I needed to count the costs of my decisions and actions. My golden handcuffs now had a plus one.

I contacted my job and explained my new reality. I was prepared to work from home, but they must have really considered the propensity for me to still perform work tasks and had an intervention. To ensure I was truly on bedrest, they came and retrieved their computer and company car. Without the company computer and car, there was no way for me to work. Not only did my new normal consist of bedrest and no work, but I also had to receive injections in my hip every week.

I always knew there was power in being still, and that the Lord always knows what we need and how to get our attention. I just never imagined having to be still for 4 months... four long months. At the time I lived on the outskirts on a lake, so I was in a very serene place as I prepared to bring life into the world. It would be in that place and during that time that God would start to reveal His plan for my life to me. I must admit, His plan did not look like my plan. The time had come for me to make a decision about re-entering the workforce. If there was one thing I was sure of, it was I did not want to go back. The thoughts and the ideas of returning to what I would describe as feeling like a caged animal, were nagging. The shine from the golden handcuffs had become dull and unappealing.

I expressed my disdain for returning to work with my husband, and he had one response -"Well don't". Wait, huh? It took me a few minutes to process his response. Did he really just tell me that I didn't have to go back to work? The answer was Yes. Entertaining the idea of not returning to the workforce was foreign to me. I never knew that was an option. I never thought I did not have to do something. I always believed you had to go to work. I had seen every woman in my life work that is what we do. But, my husband said, "Well don't".

When your mind gets the opportunity to be free and clear of the routines and obligations of the day, week, month and year, the level of clarity you can experience is unmatched. I never knew being on bedrest to prepare for the birth of my son would also serve as preparation to birth the vision God had given me. I never knew being on bedrest and allowing my husband to experience "Jessica Uncuffed", would birth a comfort in him to tell me, "Well don't".

Shortly after giving birth to a healthy baby boy, I was driving down I-20 and saw a billboard of Kenneth Shuler School of Cosmetology. I literally turned off the exit and followed the signs. Once I arrived at the building, I talked to the admissions' counselor and enrolled in cosmetology school. Was that part of my plan? No. Did I even have a plan? No. But I knew I did not want to return to that rat race of corporate America.

The day I enrolled in cosmetology school was the day I gave myself permission…permission to change my mind. I was used to feeling like I do not want to but thinking and feeling like I had to. I was determined to take that old tune off repeat. I did not even want to press the pause button. I was throwing the whole tape, cd, record away. The time had come for me to sing a new song…my song.

If I had never given myself permission to change my mind about my life and decided to rest in knowing God had a plan for my life, I would have missed the realization that I already possessed the key called purpose to unlock and release myself from the golden handcuffs.

Permission Slip

I, _____
grant myself permission to Change My Mind. I no longer must stick to my original plans. From new experiences and relationships, to establishing elevated goals and a fresh outlook, I am excited for what is to come.

_____
Your Signature

GIVE
YOURSELF
A
ROUND OF
APPLAUSE

Permission To Celebrate Myself

My husband and I recently celebrated our 20th wedding anniversary. Yes, the country girl and the city boy have been married for 20 years. We started dating in 1996 and got married in 2002.

Being the only girl, my parents spared no expense for the wedding. My mom mailed 425 invitations. Yes, 425 invitations. But we quickly learned that didn't mean we could only prepare for 425 people and their plus one to attend our wedding and reception. Some RSVPs were for 6 people. Yes, 6 people. Our wedding was quickly turning into a full out production. We got married in Georgia where the church had a capacity of about 1500 people. 1500 seats sounded like enough space for everyone to gather and celebrate our nuptials, even with 425 invitations and RSVPs anywhere from 1 to 6 people, but on our wedding day every seat in the church was taken. The church was filled with our family, our friends, and our parents' friends and friends of friends. My mentor who drove from Greenville, South Carolina got the last seat in the church way up in the balcony. Someone who actually knew us and was an active participant in loving, supporting and celebrating us, had to take a back seat to those who knew of us, had some love for us, and just wanted to see our celebration.

As I am sharing my 20th year wedding anniversary with our closest friends, I noticed that none of them knew us 20 years ago. Not a one. The person I was and the person I had become was a result of my intentional evolution. My closest friends, who I affectionally refer to as The Garden Club, are the family I chose. They have unknowingly lifted me up and held me down at my lowest points. They have helped this caterpillar develop into a beautiful butterfly and soar.

I know there is an air of mystery around me, and I am comfortable with that. But what I am not comfortable with, is being in the light. No, it is not low self-esteem or low self-worth, I just don't need the glitz and the glamour to celebrate me. I gave myself permission to celebrate me a long time ago. I have never been one to parade myself, nor expected to receive a gold star, because the fact is no matter how much I have done, there is still more to do. I still have marks to leave and people to impact. I have not learned enough. I have not shared enough.

I will sleep when I'm dead and rest when I'm rich.

The Garden Club has celebrated all of my wins. Even when I did not see the need to highlight something I had done, because I viewed it as "meeting expectations and not the exception", they made sure I felt the pats on the back from their hands and not just my own.

I used to purposely dim my light because I did not want to draw too much attention to myself, and at times, not even turn my light on. Some might say I downplayed my power. But I have learned that there is nothing to gain by shrinking or playing myself small. The poet, Marian Williamson says it best in her poem Our Deepest Fear —"Our deepest fear is not that we are inadequate. Our deepest fear is that we are powerful beyond measure. It is our light, not our darkness that most frightens us.".

I have made the decision to first turn my light on and unapologetically let it shine, all in hopes that it becomes a motivation for others to do the same.

Permission Slip

I, _____

grant myself permission to Celebrate Me. I no longer have to wait for others to recognize my accomplishments. I will give myself a gold star and I have my own confetti to throw in the air. The party of one is the best party.

_____
Your Signature

Note To Self...

Celebrate Myself

I AM
A LOT
BUT
ALSO
ENOUGH.

Permission To Give Myself Space

Family has the power to shape and mold you into the person you become, but so do friends. When I reflect on my friendships from my early childhood years through the first year of college, I notice a theme - If I had it, they had it. It was that simple. I attribute that to my grandmother and parents. I saw my grandmother take to, take in, take care of, and accept everybody. She loved everybody, and never met a stranger. My parents, who too practiced the infamous "all for one, one for all" with my friends, never let anyone go without. If I was getting my hair done, and my friend was with me, then we were getting our hair done. If I was going shopping, then my friend was going shopping. Sharing, giving, and including was a no brainer for them, which became a no brainer for me. Unbeknownst to me, it was the consistent demonstration and display of love in action that helped shaped how I loved then and how I love now. While this 4-letter word [love] is easily tossed around like an old rag doll, I know love is an action word. And while you can give without loving, you cannot love without giving. Think about that - love without giving…that is impossible. The more I think about it, that is how I built my friendships. I loved so I gave, I gave because I loved.

In elementary school and even through high school, I was a chameleon. I fit in with everybody. From athletes, preppies, nerds and hood chicks to the whites, blacks, and browns…I was that cool chick…I was Jessica. No heirs, not pretentious, just the plain ol' Jessica [don't forget I was the cool chick though]. But even with being cool, loving, and giving, how can I explain losing friendships? The truth is, I can't. I can't explain why my childhood best friend revealed she was jealous of me and abruptly ended our friendship. I can't explain how my relationship with my best friend from high school waned over time, even after we had done so much together and learned so much from each other. From writing a book to hosting seminars, I'd like to say we made an impact. I learned how to interact with people on an emotional level and all of the touchy-feely parts of a relationship from her. Watching her interact with people and their responses helped create a blueprint for relationships I currently have in my life. Don't get me wrong, I understand people can grow apart, change, and evolve, but when friendships end, it is cause for a pause. Give yourself permission to pause to access and evaluate the what, how, when, and why, and redefine how you will move and what you will allow in future friendships. Remember, setting boundaries is not for them, they are for you.

After graduating high school, I did what was expected, I went off to college. Of course, coming from a family where the importance of getting an education was instilled in us, going to college was expected, not the exception. However, the missing piece of the puzzle for me was never how or why, but where, where was I going to go to college?

There's a saying that you become what you see. While I had seen the successes, opportunities, and lifestyle provided from an education from a PWI (Public White Institution), I also couldn't turn a blind eye or deaf ear to the rich, melanated, defying the odds culture of HBCUs (Historically Black Colleges and Universities). I was fortunate enough to live and be in my formative years when the Cosby Show and A Different World dominated the television screens in Black homes. Who knew the influence of those shows would span generations. Had there been other all Black families on television before? Yes. Had there been affluent Black families on television before? Yes. Then what made The Cosby Show and A Different World so attractive? For me, it was the evidence of possibility. From graduating high school to going to a HBCU, to finding and creating friendships that were like family to finding love and creating a life ever after, I mean it was right before my eyes, every Thursday night, and I was here for it...all of it. I was Whitley Gilbert, and I was going to marry Dwayne Wayne.

Where would I go to college became the daily question. My original plan was to go to a HBCU like Howard University in Washington DC, where my oldest brother-cousin (I'll explain that relationship later) went or I would go to Hampton University in Virginia. Now, I must admit, I only take calculated risks. I only applied to Spelman College where the acceptance rate was 45%, because my mother wanted me to. I soon found out they not only wanted smart but well-rounded women. While I wasn't the smartest

27

one in high school, I knew my application package was stellar. I was voted Most Involved and Most Likely to Succeed and even had a recommendation letter from a high-ranking administrator of the school district. An invitation to spend the weekend on campus and attend the Spelman's Spelbound Experience, stole my heart, and sealed the deal. That weekend was everything I had hoped it would be and more. I felt the individuality of the student body, love from the faculty, and the sisterhood. I was on my way to creating my own Whitley Gilbert experience. It felt right.

Whew chile, from day one, college did just what it was supposed to do, broadened me. I saw varying levels of wealth. I knew students living in dorm rooms without air conditioning to apartments in Buckhead (an affluent uptown district of Atlanta, Georgia). I went from watching Rudy Huxtable (Keisha Knight Pulliam) on my television screen to walking on the same campus. I went from reading about Bill Cosby's "real" daughters and son (not the Huxtables) to walking the campus with one of them. You talk about surreal. Here I was going from cool chick, one of the few Black girls in my classes Jessica, to now being fully immersed into a culture that was rich and full of people who looked like me and sounded like me…and I loved it. Was it intimidating? Absolutely. While it felt good being myself, I did wonder how do I act adequately black? Yes, that's a thing – acting black enough was and is a reality for so many, and I was one of those people. How will I create new friendships? Will I be accepted? Will I be rejected? Those thoughts ran rampant in my brain, but deep down I knew I was a good, correction, a great friend and my tribe would eventually find me. Even though I wasn't in search of sisterhood I was able to find my circle of friends in the dorms and my Dwayne Wayne was right downtown attending Georgia Tech. I know it probably sounds too good to be true, but it was a dream come true for me. I had the best of both worlds…again. Looking back, I know I did not take advantage of the full college experience. One might say I missed out because I didn't branch out, but my response would be I didn't know to *want to* do "stuff". Afterall I was getting my education, hanging out with my boyfriend who was also my best friend, I had found my tribe, so quite frankly, I was good. I didn't miss out on anything. The reality is I had the college experience I was supposed to have. In the midst of entering a new chapter of life and discovering who I was and was becoming, I gave myself permission to give myself space…space to form my own circle of influence and create my own experience…on my own terms.

Permission Slip

I, _____

grant myself permission to Give Myself Space. I no longer must remain attached to what and who no longer serves the person I am, and the person I am becoming. Space allows room for growth, and I am excited for what will bloom.

_____
Your Signature

Note To Self...

YOU DON'T
HAVE TO
THROW A
STONE AT
EVERY
BARKING
DOG.

Permission To Protect My Peace

Woof! Woof!..the universal sound of a barking dog. When heard, someone's natural instinct is to look in the direction of the sound. Depending on the direction of the sound and if it sounds loud and forceful or faint and soft, determines the next internal question, "Is it loose or behind a fence?".

Barking dogs are a part of life. They either bark to make you aware of their presence to get your attention, warn you about danger or to let you know they see you. If you hear barking repeatedly, it becomes easier each time to ignore its existence. But, if the sound is new or infrequent, human inclination is to give it some attention.

I've had some barking dogs in my day. They may not have had 4 legs, but their intention was to get my attention. They wanted to distract me from what I was supposed to be doing. Take me off my course. Life is filled with barking dogs and I have had to protect myself in every area of it. I gave myself permission to protect my peace.

My grandmother used to tell me that I did not have to throw a stone at every barking dog, meaning I did not have to pay attention or even address everything that tried to distract me, even when it looked like it could attack or cause harm. Me paying attention or me addressing the distraction could be a waste of my precious resources – time, energy, or money. I was better off reserving my resources for times and situations that mattered.

I've evolved to the point in my life where I unapologetically protect my peace. I value myself enough to know that I can not be everything to everybody. I have always been the friend that if life took a toll and left you standing in the rain, I would come where you were, but I'm going to have an umbrella and we are going to walk back inside…together. I'm not going to watch you cry or just throw an umbrella out to you.

But in even being a friend, I had to learn that I am not anyone's source. Just because I could help, did not mean it was always appropriate for me to step in and assist. I have become intentional

33

about discerning when God wants to use me to be the vessel by which He blesses someone, versus me having a knee-jerk reaction to help. These situations are distractions too. They keep me from doing what I am supposed to be doing. Life continues to bring new opportunities that I have been preparing for. I have to protect myself from feelings of guilt about moving forward and being blessed, instead of trying to want for others what they don't want for themselves.

As I continue to evolve as woman, I have to be intentional about not allowing anyone or any circumstance to change who I am. I am a generous, nurturing, and caring person. I know I overwhelm people with my giving as I recognize I am a tsunami of generosity. I strive to be who God has called me to be. I know situations and circumstances will come where I am hurt or taken advantage of, but I can't become inaccessible. I refuse to cut myself off from who God called me to be. I stand firm in knowing He will take care of all situations and forever cover me, so I don't have to change who I am.

Permission Slip

I, _____

grant myself permission to Protect My Peace. I accept that I cannot be everything to everybody. I am a resource used by God to be a blessing to His people. I will be mindful of how I use my resources of time, energy and money.

_____
Your Signature

Note To Self...

GET
UNCOMFORTABLE
BEING
COMFORTABLE

Permission To Stretch Myself

I love sports. I love sports probably as much as I love hair and I love hair, and all things beauty. The great part about sports is the ability to witness how an athlete evolves from one season to the next. As a fan, it is easy for me to sit in the stands and critique an athlete's performance, identifying all the ways they could have better performed and fended off their opponent. I've watched sports long enough to know that some victories are not obtained because the opposing team or athlete out performed the other, sometimes it is in those crunch moments that the victory is won because a decision was made to change a play or stretch themselves beyond what was comfortable and familiar. Life is like sports, you have to be willing to stretch yourself beyond what is comfortable, popular and easily accessible.

I believe one of the most important decisions I have made for myself was the decision to evolve. Evolve is an action word that means to change or develop slowly into a better state. With only six letters – 3 vowels and 3 consonants, it commands the same type of attention a well-dressed woman commands when she walks into a room without saying one word.

Life is forever evolving. You are either growing or dying, evolving or deteriorating. There is not such thing as standing still. No one makes a decision to deteriorate, but if you are not taking care of yourself or investing in the vision, purpose, abilities and skills you have been blessed with, you are making a decision to deteriorate.

For most people, working jobs they don't like or doing things they don't enjoy just to collect a paycheck is their way of life. For years I was most people. I spent 8 years, 8 long years doing what I like to refer to as the responsible thing to do. I went to college, earned my degree and got a good paying job in corporate America. I followed the implied blueprint for my life…that no one consulted me about. But here is where I am different from most people, I always knew very succinctly that I love doing hair! I love helping a woman see themselves in a way they had only envisioned or hoped for.

The love of doing hair is never just about hair. While people think it is trivial, it is really a ministry. The capability to change the way a woman looks at herself, the way she sees herself creates a movement that can span a lifetime. The confidence that is unleashed within her, is unmatched, and cannot be contained. From the way she walks, talks, performs on her job, to the way she shows up as an amazing wife, mother, sister and friend, can change the trajectory of her life. Doing hair is like Michael Jackson's song – Wanna Be Startin' Somethin'.

Having a son played an integral point in my life. Even as an infant he caused me to move past my fears, doubts, and insecurities. I made a decision to follow my dreams and enroll into cosmetology school. No more silencing my dreams to live out the Responsible Thing to Do Blueprint designed for my life. I only get one life and it's not a dress rehearsal. This was not a practice game or scrimmage. This was the real thing. And just like we expect our favorite athletes to show up and do their best, there was someone waiting for me to show up, but I could not show up for anyone else, if I did not show up for myself first. Was it easy? No. Was it worth it? Yes, yes indeed. The beauty of becoming a mother is the responsibility to raising a child to follow their dreams and to become the best version of themselves. How was I going to raise my son to follow his dreams and I was suffocating mine?

Caution, there is a thing about making decisions, there are people who will not understand or agree with you. When making a decision for yourself you cannot seek validation. People won't get it, and you have to be okay. If you live by people's applause, you will die by their silence.

Making a decision to stretch yourself beyond what is comfortable, familiar and popular can be lonely. It was lonely for me. Although family and friends now say how proud they are of me, there were and still are moments when their silence is deafening. I know leaving corporate America to go to cosmetology school was a shock for those persons connected and even those familiar with me. How would they be able to explain to their friends or even themselves, me leaving a lucrative 6-figure salary to do hair? How would they brag about me if all I was doing was hair? Did I expect them to get it or understand? No. I had quickly come to the realization of one thing – people won't get it!

In reality, it is hard for people to celebrate someone doing what they wish they had the courage to do. When you have a front row seat watching someone else say "yes" to themselves, that creates a mirror reflecting the countless times "no" became the chosen option.

Faith without work is dead, and I was living now more than ever. I was in cosmetology school every night from 5 to 10pm for one year. Adding mother to list of responsibilities, I admittedly was no spring chicken. Everyone in my class was about 10 years younger than me, but hey it was my time.

Being new to Columbia, South Carolina, in looking around I did not see any beauty salon options I would pursue after graduation. I was finally preparing to live out my dream as a licensed cosmetologist and just anything was not going to do. Wherever I was going to launch my career and share my skills needed to meet certain requirements. I understood my work. I understood what a pair of sheers in my hand created and produced. Money, yes, but I am speaking of women with a new pep in their step, a restored self-awareness and self-worth. I understood the value in gifting women hope to trust themselves again. A new hairstyle was not just a new look, but a new look on life.

As they say, necessity is the mother of invention. It was obviously birthing season. God was doing a new thing and I was ready for it…all of it. From birthing my baby boy to birthing my new beauty brand business, The Pynk Butterfly – Where Beauty Meets Evolution.

I wanted to create an environment where I wanted to be in and to practice my craft. Being in business was never my goal, I just wanted to do hair, and be in the beauty industry. I didn't need my name on the marquee or in lights. It was never about seeing Jessica's Bump and Curl on a billboard on I-20. It was always about the brand, never about me.

I didn't wait for graduation day to arrive before I started

40

preparations to launch The Pynk Butterfly, because I wanted a place for me and my classmates to work that would provide an experience unlike any other in Columbia, South Carolina.

I brought my 8 years of corporate America experience to the planning table and created what I believed would elevate not only the Columbia community but the expectations and experience of seasoned and new stylists.

The Pynk Butterfly was destined to soar and change the game. Did stepping into the business of launching my own beauty scare me? Yes. But more importantly, it stretched me. It caused me to lay by the side the fears, disappointments, expectations of others and pick up the promises, purpose and provisions God had provided for me.

Since I launched the salon as soon as I graduated cosmetology school, no one in the salon had been in the industry so I had to seek mentorship and guidance outside of the salon. If I was going to keep evolving, it was necessary. Forming and cultivating those relationships aided in my growth as a boss.

Being labeled a boss is usually associated with a negative connotation, but I was a boss from a cooperative position, where vision and leadership were served as the main course at my table. Was it hard to embrace the title Pynk Boss? Yes, but it was part of my evolution, and inevitable part if I was going to continue to stretch myself and walk in my purpose.

I have not worked a single day since leaving corporate America. I get to go play in the sandbox every day I walk into the salon. Why did I deny myself this freedom for so long? I'll never know, but I know giving myself permission to stretch and reach beyond what was safe, familiar and comfortable, opened the doors to my purpose.

Permission Slip

I, _____

grant myself permission to Stretch Myself. I will no longer confine myself to what, who or where is comfortable and familiar. I will stretch beyond the limitations I have placed on myself.

_____
Your Signature

Note To Self...

Stretch Myself

LET
YOUR
LIGHT
SHINE
BRIGHT

Permission To Remove My Mask

Covid-19 changed the game for every person and every industry in the world. The way people worked, shopped, sought health care, traveled, worshipped and bought cars; it was no longer business as usual. In fact, it did not matter what was in your bank account, what degree was hanging on your wall, what position you held, how many letters you had behind your name or even the color of your skin, COVID was here and normal was nowhere to be found. No privilege cards would allow you to be exempt from the impact of COVID. From mask mandates and social distancing to virus tracing and quarantining, if there was ever going to be the discovery of the new normal, it had to start with a pivot in life and business.

The Pynk Butterfly had to close its doors like every other business. There was no human resource department to call and inquire about being compensated during the pandemic. That wasn't an option in this industry. This business only gets paid if the doors are open. Even with everything closed, the bills didn't stop, there was still overhead that had to be paid. The landlord wanted his rent. SCE&G still wanted payment for the electric bill. But there was no money coming in, and life was still going, even if it had a curfew, with a mask, staying 6 feet apart. I needed to make a decision, actually some tough decisions, so I did what I always do when challenges arise - I took a moment, well two moments to get quiet to sit back and really look at the situation that I was facing and sought wisdom, not counsel. Seeking wisdom is different than seeking counsel. While sometimes counsel can be beneficial, when there is a decision needed to be made, that could alter the trajectory of my life, I seek God.

There's a limited number of people who were qualified to advise me about The Pynk Butterfly. At the time, the concept of The Pynk Butterfly had never been done before. No one was creating luxury beauty salons in Columbia, SC. No one was intentional about creating an experience when women got their beauty needs addressed. There was no one who had ever been where I wanted to go, nor been where I had been. Yes, it is cool to receive pats and rubs on the back, like the old school church back rubs that were usually accompanied with the peppermint, or someone saying baby, it's going to be okay, like Method Man and Mary J. but in those moments, true life altering moments I had to seek The One who made me, The One who forgave me, The One who told me I was his own. I knew and I know there is nothing I could present to God that he did not already know and had not already worked out. As the old song goes, while I was trying to figure it out, He had already worked it out.

The interesting part about having my business shut down and with no money coming in, all while coping and navigating through a pandemic, is that I couldn't cry. I honestly don't even know when it's appropriate for me to cry. I mean really, when is it appropriate for a strong woman to have a vulnerable moment? I was raised not seeing emotions expressed externally. No one ever said it, but it was demonstrated that you keep your game face on and never let them see you sweat. Like so many women, I had to fix my face take a deep breath and begin to breathe. Truth be told I was not only sweating from crying privately but sweating from wearing two masks, the one I had been trained to wear as I walk the walk and talk the talk and the one that was mandated due to COVID. Is it just me, or is it getting hot in here (in my Nelly voice)? I have been the rock for so many, but a rock needs a rock as well. I portray that I have it all figured out because, otherwise a magnifying glass could be held over my insecurities.

The time had come, it was time to pivot. I couldn't do business the same way, not with COVID being an uninvited guest in our world, with no hint of leaving soon. I took inventory of all the resources, skills, people, ideas and creativity that I possessed and realized God had already given me the answer. He had already shown me the next step. It was going to be up to me to step up, step out and remove my mask. I had been dimming my light long enough and the world needed my shine, literally and figuratively.

In 2006, while still in cosmetology school I began creating my own hair care products. I had foam wrap, shine and now my famous B.O.S.S. oil. The shine had such a distinctive aroma that it marketed itself. I would spray it and clients would immediately ask, "What's that smell?". I never marketed the products publicly because I was fearful of how people would receive them. Sounds silly, but my products were like my babies and just like a mother and her children, she thinks they're beautiful and amazing, but never sure if everyone else will think the same. That thought created fear and I hid behind it for protection for far too long.

Much of my clientele totally relied on The Pynk Butterfly products for their haircare needs, so much so many didn't have shampoo in their home. If any shampooing was to happen, it was to happen at only The Pynk Butterfly. Recognizing the need of my clients and needing to generate income, to pivot in my business I created quarantine kits. Although I had my own products, I used products from other companies that I had in inventory and just added The Pynk Butterfly shine and boss oil to the kits. Even with my own signature supplies, I don't know why I did not use them in the kits. But when I say something really woke up in me, I mean it. I had slept on me long enough. I [finally] started making Pynk Butterfly home maintenance kits, using only Pynk Butterfly products…that I've had all along. No need to shake your head because I am shaking mine. I decided to be an active participant in my evolution…using something I already had, but no one could see because it was masked behind fear.

COVID has taken the lives of people and the life out of many businesses. It has also caused people to pause and assess what they already possess. Wearing a mask was not new for me, but COVID caused me to realize that it was time to give myself permission to remove my mask and shine like a boss, the Pynk Boss that I am.

Permission Slip

I, _____
grant myself permission to Remove My Mask. I have hidden behind fear for far too long. I will silence the thoughts and ideas that try to keep me hidden. It is time for me to step up and step out. It is time for my light to shine.

_____
Your Signature

Note To Self...

Remove My Mask

MAKE
AND
KEEP YOUR
APPOINTMENT
WITH
YOURSELF

Permission To Prioritize Myself

There's an old saying that you can't pour from an empty cup. Well either my cup was part of a magic show kit, you know the ones that have the ability to make things appear as though they are when they are not, or my cup had an invisible hose attached to it, so it filled up on its own, because to this day like many people, I don't know how I showed up for everyone else for so long, except for one person, the most important person - myself.

When I think about it, I have got to ask myself, -"How was I not on my own to-do list?", "How did I keep missing appointments with myself?", "How did my needs and wants become simply an option?". Just thinking about it opens the floodgates of emotion. No, I didn't become this way over night. Life experiences can trigger questions that may lead to some harsh realities. Interestingly enough, it only took a 10-minute conversation to undo what I envisioned would have been a life-long friendship. Talk about a day to remember. It would become what I would like to refer to as a transformational moment a teaching moment a tough pill to swallow moment, but it was my moment. It would become the moment which created a shift within myself that caused me to recognize and understand that friendships are expensive, emotionally expensive.

Just like high-end designer bags are nice to have and make you feel good, they are not necessary. Coming into the understanding that friendships are a luxury is why I had to choose to spend my emotional currency on me.

Things could have been handled differently but I now understand that placement at the bottom of a "things to-do list" is the list owner's choice and is also a reference of priority. And as much as I believed I was a priority, in reality I was a nonfactor.

Being a creature of habit, usually I would have put on my cape, swooped in as Captain Jessica and assumed the position - emotionally, financially, intellectually or geographically to "fix it". And in true Jessica form I did go into my "fix it" mode, but this time it was different. Instead of going into my "fix it" mode for another, I went into "fix it" mode for myself. I made how I felt and my needs the priority. I quickly became very clear of the fact that no one was going to swoop in and save me. The fact is I had to save myself. I had to pick myself up and figure it out.

Talk about uncharted territory, I was not used to tending to me. But this time, something broke, something finally broke. I didn't mask it. I didn't try to numb it. I had to try something different. Doing nothing was not an option. It was time for me to feel what I was feeling. It was time to focus on me. It was time to fix Jessica.

All my life I had to fight. No, not in the physical sense, but what I would arguably suggest is worse is the internal fight - mentally and emotionally. My whole life had been spent not letting other people down, which unknowingly meant I was placing myself at the bottom of my own "to-do list". Without ever saying it, I had made myself a nonfactor, which meant for years I had done to myself what I came to despise others for doing to me. But this time, this time it was on me to make the shift. This time I had to make the choice to not let myself down.

The time had come to make sure I kept that same energy as I committed and focused on myself the way I had committed to other people.

Establishing and enforcing boundaries was only a problem for people who were inconvenienced by them. Being mindful that boundaries are not for others but for myself began to feel good, really good. From structured appointment blocks for my beauty clients to a weekly non-negotiable standing appointment with my masseuse, unapologetically doing what I wanted and needed to do, removed the guilt of prioritizing me.

Permission Slip

I, _____

grant myself permission to Prioritize Myself. I am committed to making and keeping appointments with myself. I am no longer preserving anyone's feelings at the cost of my own. I am a priority and not an option, to myself or anyone who has the luxury of being connected to me.

_____
Your Signature

Note To Self...

Prioritize Myself

TRUST
HIS STILL
QUIET
VOICE

Permission To Trust God's Plan

Growing up I heard sermons, memorized scriptures, recited Easter speeches and sang hymns. I accepted Jesus Christ as my personal Lord and Savior at the tender age of 8. I still remember stepping out into the aisle and walking to the front, to join church and to get baptized. I did not tell anybody, because it was in the moment, and I just felt led to do it. Now that I think about it, I surprised everybody when I stood up and stepped into the aisle. That was the day I gave myself permission to trust God.

As I grew and matured in my faith, God became more real to me. I found myself resting on the words to songs like My Soul Has Been Anchored in The Lord, Amazing Grace or His Eye Is on the Sparrow. Going through the ups and downs of life and living long enough, the lyrics to those songs began to have a different meaning. I can recall within my own life how I was lost, but He found me, how I was blind, but He allowed me to see, and how He watches over me. He consistently reminds me that He will not leave me nor forsake me and that provides a peace that surpasses all understanding.

Life is filled with making decisions, but society has consequently created an "initiative-suppressed" thinking within people. It is unfortunate, but no one wants to take the initiative. No one wants to step out and try things on their own. No one wants to be the first to pursue an alternative way. No one wants to go down the untraveled path. Whether it is out of fear of being wrong, getting into trouble, being seen as an imposter or if it is because there is nobody to blame if it does not work out as planned, people are living beneath their potential and privilege.

It is in the moments of uncertainty that I find myself relying on God's still quiet voice to lead and direct me. It is in these moments I give myself permission to trust Him and His plan. Regardless of how it looks and how it feels, I permit myself to trust Him. Has it always been easy? No. But it did become easier once I reminded myself of who I am to Him and the promises He made to me. I am the apple of His eye. I rest in the lyrics – I was blind, but now I see.

God is such a gentleman. He was not going to push Himself into your life. For me to receive salvation, I had to choose to believe in Him. I had to choose to believe that He died on the cross and was resurrected. **I had to invite Him in.** I gave myself permission to trust God and the plan He had for my life. I had to give myself permission to allow Him to make himself real to me and know that He will always take care of me. What did I have to lose? I saw how far I could get myself with my abilities, so why not turn complete control of my life to Him and trust His plan.

It is true if we allow God to have control in our lives, everything becomes better and greater. He exceeds anything we could ask, think, or imagine.

Permission Slip

I, _____
grant myself permission to Trust
God's Plan. I am no longer bound
to the plans and timelines I
created for my life. I will trust
God's plans and rest in knowing
He has already worked it out, so I
do not need to try and figure it
out.

_____
Your Signature

Note To Self...

Trust God's Plan

DREAM
BIG
AND
DREAM
OFTEN

Permission To Dream BIG

My boyfriend turned amazing husband for the past 20 years sold me a dream while we were young in the streets of Atlanta, Georgia. He introduced me to The Alexandria. The Alexandria were brownstones in a gated townhouse community in North Atlanta's sought-after upscale Buckhead-Lenox neighborhood. The cost for some of them were well over $700,000. I grew up where everybody had nice things and was not a foreign concept, but no one was balling. In my mind I wanted to be Whitley Gilbert and marry Dwayne Wayne. I would be the armpiece, the stay-at-home wife, the philanthropist, so taking a tour of The Alexandra is where my "would be" met "could be", face-to-face. He was selling a dream and I was buying it.

I would not be considered wise if I did not understand that dreams required sacrifices. As we traveled the road to achieving our dream of buying the Alexandria, we were also traveling the road called entrepreneurship. We found ourselves investing and reinvesting back into The Pynk Butterfly brand. Without having to allocate funds to the business, we probably could have owned two or three Alexandrias. If I had it my way, I would have been the trophy wife, living in the Alexandria and building The Pynk Butterfly brand. Since we had not reached that goal yet, I decided not to be the trophy wife and utilize my skills and ability to attain my dreams. Why wait when you can participate.

Throughout life that dream had always been dangled and teased, but my husband was the one that made it appear reachable and attainable. If I was going to take the time to dream, I might as well dream big.

My husband told me something that I will never forget. He said, " You are great and amazing, but so am I. I chose you and continue too every day. I am not here because I have to, I choose to". It is his quiet strength that gets me every time. Between the two of us, he is the dreamer, and he allows me to dream. He always opened my mind and fathom to possibilities. I never wanted to own a business, but it would be his discovery of a space and my husband saying, "This could be your first salon", that the floodgates of possibilities would fill my mind. Me owning my own salon had never crossed my mind. I would have been fine behind a chair at JCPenney, if the environment was conducive to my success and provided the experience I wanted my clients to have. But the more I sat with the idea of owning my own, the dreams became bigger.

A lot of people know what's inside of them and what their gifts are, but it is what happens on the outside that keeps people stuck and playing small. Sadly, I was a lot of those people. I was the chapter president, had the t-shirt and the mug. Why was playing small, playing by other people's rules, and being off the grid somehow making me think I was doing myself a favor? Dreaming big was required if I was ever going to fill the shoes that had my name on them. I had to decide to be the gift that God intended me to be and use the gift.

When I decided to open my flagship salon, The Pynk Butterfly Signature Salon and Spa, I dreamed of creating an environment where beauty professionals could feel what I felt in corporate America - taken care of. From vacation time to insurance, all they had to do was show up. The Pynk Butterfly paid for marketing and was responsible for getting clients in the seats. We even had a dress code schedule. The idea was to promote consistency and uniformity. I didn't want people to have to hustle to make ends meet, thus my reason for putting stylist on salaries, some over what they deserved. I truly wanted to give them an experience that they had never dreamed of, or thought was possible in our industry. And there lies the problem, I wanted something more for them than they wanted for themselves. I realize I was asking people to create and thrive in a spa environment; many had never been to a spa and executing a dream they had never even seen. The idea behind creating a corporate experience in the salon was simple, all they had to do was show up.

Business is networking and relationships. Not only was I building a beauty brand based in Columbia, South Carolina, The Pynk Butterfly was spreading its wings to another continent, Africa. Talk about enlarging my territory. I could not have dreamed this big on the best pillowtop mattress, wearing my The Pynk Butterfly satin bonnet.

While in Johannesburg at Mandela Square selling exotic hair and to open a salon, word spread that we were there and somehow ended up on the rooftop sitting with the King's son - the prince and his 2 wives. One of the wives was thinking of gifting hair as a wedding favor for the next wedding because the prince was preparing to take another bride.

Thinking back on that time in Johannesburg truly causes me to pause because so much favor was bestowed and deployed during that trip. According to Proverbs 18:16 – "A man's gift makes room for him and brings him before great men". Great men and woman are not just Kings and Queens in the royalty sense, but kings and queens of their industry, community and home.

When you decide to not simply use your gift, but be the gift, it will cause attention to come, and you will be able to help other people and touch many more lives. You have to make the decision not to play small and keep to yourself.

Dreaming big as you use and become your gift requires you to share your gift. I purposely dimmed my light because I did not want to draw attention to myself. But I knew I had a responsibility to not only myself but to the voices and people assigned to what I had to say and teach. The same way I looked up and learned from people is the same way people look me up to learn from me. It's not only a responsibility, it is a privilege. Whether I ever see them or not, there are eyes watching my actions and ears listening to me speak. If I am going to be the gift, use the gift, pursue the gift and share the gift, I have to give myself permission to dream big. I will never know how my life sparked someone else to not only dream, but to dream BIG.

Permission Slip

I, _____

grant myself permission to Dream BIG. I will not become scared of what I see, but inspired to take the limits off and elevate my expectations. Better, greater and bigger are coming!

_____
Your Signature

Note To Self...

Dream BIG

GOD IS THE ONLY ONE WHO CAN MULTIPLY BY SUBTRACTION

Permission To Lose to Win

"It's not what you say, it's what you do". While you may have heard that saying or something similar countless times, I challenge you to consider this, "It's not only what you do, but what you don't do". Not making a decision is making a decision. Making a decision can be the difference between life and death, wealth and poverty, wellness and illness, losing and winning.

If we lived on islands, our decisions would have minimal to no effect on anyone else beside ourselves, but since we don't, making a decision to push past the fears, insecurities and uncertainties of being an entrepreneur, and leading by example changed the trajectory for my brand and me.

Before graduating cosmetology school, I launched The Pynk Butterfly beauty brand. I know that was pretty ambitious but looking back I would not have done it any other way. My first salon opened in 2006. It was in a cute, small brickhouse in West Columbia, South Carolina. It was called The Pynk Butterfly Hair Studio. It was the perfect setup for a perfect beginning. Even with limited parking, it was perfect.

The Bible says in Zechariah 4:10 – "Do not despise these small beginnings, for the Lord rejoices to see work begin...". Obviously the Lord was up to something. Greater was coming and I was ready for it. Before we knew it, The Pynk Butterfly Hair Studio had outgrown the space. Business was growing, and The Pynk Butterfly was becoming what I had envisioned, the go to for beauty! Growth was not only taking place in The Pynk Butterfly, but it was also taking place in me. The Pynk Boss, as I was affectionately referred to as, was stretching and growing. I decided to take a leap and elevate The Pynk Butterfly in its fullness, in the way I wanted to see it. And that's when The Pynk Butterfly Signature Salon and Spa was birthed. We were something like The Jeffersons - George and Louise, moving on up.

Envision living in a studio apartment then moving to a 5-bedroom 5-bathroom house, talk about an upgrade. The Pynk Butterfly

Signature Salon and Spa was 10,000 square foot beautiful space in Richland Mall in Columbia, South Carolina. It had areas for hair prep, nails, spa, estheticians, and masseuses. It was beautiful. We hosted events like neo-soul Sundays and Pynk at Night. It was everything I envisioned for The Pynk Butterfly brand at that time.

Over time the structure of the mall began deteriorating and the air conditioner was going out. Guess who had to foot the bill for the air conditioner? Yes, The Pynk Butterfly. Replacing an air condition unit for a home is one thing, but for a 10,000 square foot workspace was a different story, and I wasn't reading that book. The estimated replacement cost was over $50,000. But that's not where the problems stopped. Whenever it rained, it rained inside the mall too. With holes in the ceilings and the need to purchase a $50,000 air conditioner unit, guess what time it was? It was time to go. A large part of me didn't want to let it go. Silly, right? I was burdened with my perception of what other's perceptions would be. What would people think? What will they say about closing this big, beautiful location to move to something smaller? In life and business, you're supposed to upgrade not down grade, so I thought.

I know I should not have cared, but I knew I had an audience who wanted to see me succeed and an audience who wanted to see me fail. While the support of those rooting for me to succeed was obvious through their actions and words, those who wanted me to fail was just as obvious. Silence speaks volume, and I wish I could have pressed mute, but there were too many missed opportunities to prove me wrong. I believed closing The Pynk Butterfly Signature Salon and Spa would give them front row seats to the show they wanted to see, titled "You Failed, and We Knew You Would".

I questioned God. I did. I could not understand why He would allow me to finally build and experience what I envisioned for The Pynk Butterfly, only for me to close it down. What I didn't understand at the time was that God was up to something again. I had to make the decision to trust Him and His process. Over time He revealed to me that The Pynk Butterfly Signature Salon and Spa was a steppingstone to other things and other blessings, blessings that were bigger and greater. Bigger and greater didn't necessarily mean in size, but it did mean in impact. I can now look back and see how it was a necessary step in the evolution of The Pynk Butterfly and me.

God requiring closure of the Richland Mall location was an external example of what He was doing internally. He was closing doors to thoughts of failure, doubt, and other's perceptions. I had to lose the limits I had placed on God, the brand and myself. I had to give myself permission to lose to win, if I was ever going to experience the magnanimous blessings God had in store for my brand and me.

Permission Slip

I, _____
grant myself permission to Lose to Win. I understand I can no longer continue to carry the emotional baggage. I have to lose the limitations I have placed on God and myself to see and understand what lies ahead positions me to win.

_____
Your Signature

Note To Self...

Lose to Win

OPTIONS
OVER
OPTICS

Permission To Pursue What I Love

Life is filled with countless moments of when you discover that you don't know, what you don't know. It is in those defining moments that cause you to question the experiences you missed out on that could have exposed you to a whole new world of opportunity. I wish I had known sooner in my life that I had options, options on how I could live my life.

As the old saying goes, your cousins are you first friends. Growing up, I was the only child for a long time, meaning I didn't become a big sister until I was 8 years old. But, I had brothers. I know that does not make sense, so let me explain. Before I officially became a big sister, my cousins were my brothers. We did everything together. We were treated like siblings. We loved each other like siblings. We were considered the 5 jewels in my grandmother's crown. We even used each other's decisions as blueprints like siblings. Blueprints? Yes, blueprints. Just like most families, the oldest "sibling" set the bar and expectations for the younger "siblings" to follow. And boy oh boy did my oldest brother set the bar. You talk about expectations? I clearly needed to make some personal/internal adjustments, and they needed to be made quickly. Not only did my oldest brother go to Howard University for undergrad and Harvard for his PhD, but the second oldest attend Oklahoma and Georgia Tech to earn his degrees.

The expectation for our family was established by my grandmother. She was a trailblazer while raising her own children, and those generational principles were passed down and instilled in us. So, as I grew up, I thought you were supposed to go to grade school, high school and then go to college. After you graduated college, you started your career. Call it the responsible thing to do, but I had seen the benefits of following the blueprint and the quality of life it provided. The things I always wanted to have; I could now buy. The places I wanted to travel to; I could now visit. The knowledge of doing what was expected; I had accomplished. But at some point in life, I reviewed life's receipts and realized that the things I bought, the places I had gone and the experiences I had put on hold, all had a cost.

I wish I had known that pursuing my passion was an option. I had carried the weight of my passion for hair since I was a child. From doing the dolls' hair I would receive at Christmas time as gifts, to the little girls in my grandmother's neighborhood, where I would visit in the summer and braid their hair, I have had hair in my hands my whole life. I always knew I wanted to do hair, but not becoming a degreed professional was never an option for me. Passions were fine to have, but I was conditioned to believe that professional development paid the bills and painted the picture of success.

I knew the people around me had passions, but they didn't make pursuing those passions look differently from working. For example, my dad loved music. I never saw him throw on a jacket and play in a rock band on the weekends for fun, instead we moved to Florida so he could earn his PhD in music theory from Florida State University. My mom loved helping people. Not only did she become a registered nurse, but she continued her studies to earn an MBA. I had numerous examples around me that highlighted professions over passions, but deep down I knew that is how my story would end.

I finally gave myself permission to pursue what I loved. I chose options over optics. Being concerned about what other people thought or felt could no longer be the hinge in the door that kept it from swinging my way and opening up the world of opportunity. I loved hair and was not afraid to shout it from the roof top. Every woman in my family valued their appearance, from the crown of their heads to the soles of their feet. They understood the power in maintaining their hair. Needless to say, having to share my decision to pursue what I loved, was met trepidation. The sighs, eye rolls or radio silence, did not stop this ship from sailing. I knew what I wanted to do. I knew what I needed to do. I knew what I was supposed to do. I have come to know that my obedience and sacrifice to the call that was on my life would help ignite someone else's self-discovery of needing to give themselves permission to pursue their passion.

Hair, so simple yet so complex. The anguish and the toil many women put themselves through when it comes the texture of their

74

hair, how to wear or style their hair is often wrapped in permission. The perceived need to get permission to change their hair or how to wear their hair is deep rooted. Whether it is from childhood experiences, society's standards or self-esteem, many women feel permission is needed. A woman does need permission from herself.

Whether it is a profession, passion, or project, give yourself permission permission to pursue what you love.

Permission Slip

I, _____

grant myself permission to Pursue What I Love. I will no longer be confined to familiarity. I will take the lid off the can of possibilities and opportunities to discover and pursue what I love.

_____
Your Signature

Note To Self...

Pursue What I Love

THERE
IS
BEAUTY
IN THE
EVOLUTION

Permission To Evolve

First comes love, then comes marriage, then comes the baby in the baby carriage. I remember singing those words growing up with my friends, not knowing that they would become the sequence of my life. I have the blessing of finding love early in life. My love for hair was discovered through what may have been seen as unintentional experiences, but they were little breadcrumbs that would lead me to my purpose.

Growing up, my dad would take me to get my hair done. No, he would not come in and sit in the chairs reading Home and Garden magazines or fall asleep out of pure boredom, but he would drive up to the front door of the beauty salon, hand me a check and I would get out of the car and open the door to my wonderland.

The beauty salon, yes beauty salon, not beauty shop was where I saw the magic happen. I would spend hours observing how people arrived and how people departed, and how it was never the same. They always left better than they came. There was more confidence, more smiles, more laughter. It was like a reset button had been pushed. I would observe how the staff interacted with each client and each other. Observation and experiences truly became my teachers.

Yes, I was the girl growing up that used to braid the kids' hair in the neighborhood, who became the girl in the dorms doing everybody's hair and makeup. I might not have experienced all of the "college stuff" during my days on the campus of Spelman College, but I made sure my circle of friends looked good. I would like to think they were my first glimpse of what was to come…marriage.

Before two people decide to get married, usually they have spent a significant amount of time together. They have taken the time to get to know one another. From discovering each other's likes and dislikes, goals and desires, to interacting with each other's friends and family. Before a person decides to entertain the idea of marriage, they are usually open to a myriad of experiences and encounters that aid them in discovering their desires, detailing their goals, and defining their non-negotiables.

I know marriage is a big commitment. It is not anything that should be entered into lightly or without counsel. While most little girls were and are encouraged to think about their wedding day, many of us go so far as to assign it a deadline. We begin to plan our lives around it. With no idea or regard for what God has prepared for us or the experiences he desires and needs us to have, we have already scheduled the "out of office" email response. We do not want to hear it If the wedding does not happen according to "our" timeline. We are not even open to taking a detour…God arranged detour.

That was me. I took a detour before getting married. I traveled down the road that led to the front door of corporate America. I neatly tucked my love for hair in a nice box and placed it in the closet with the tailored suits, designer handbags and shoes I wore as a unit manager of hundreds of stores. I did not know that spending the next 8 years working for Philip Morris USA, was also business and networking training for entrepreneurship. The business acumen I developed was part of the foundation I needed to stand on to build my business.

Shortly after becoming pregnant, I was placed on bedrest. I spent July through November at home before welcoming the birth of my beautiful baby boy. With maternity leave stretched out through March, I had plenty of time and mental space to talk with God and think with clarity. It became very clear, and I decided I did not want to return to the workforce. With two words, "Well don't", my husband voiced his support. Never in a million years did I think not returning to work was an option, but it was abundantly clear that I was evolving. What had always been, was now being challenged by what could be. The opportunity to explore the possibilities was freeing. The caged animal had been released.

Shortly after having my baby boy, I was driving down I-20 and had an experience that would lead to the marriage of my passion and purpose. I saw a billboard for The Kenneth Shuler School of Cosmetology and followed the street signs until I ended up in the admission's office. It was happening finally. The time had come to go in my closet, open the nice box and take out my passion…my love for hair. The training I received for the next year from The Kenneth Shuler School of Cosmetology united with my love for hair was an undeniable union. The skills developed and the relationships formed were part of the blueprint being created to not only transform the haircare services offered in Columbia, South Carolina, but to transform the beauty industry.

While still in cosmetology school, but before graduation, I became pregnant again. Although it was an unplanned pregnancy, it was exactly what I needed and wanted. I birthed The Pynk Butterfly brand. I knew that once I became a licensed cosmetologist I would want to provide a quintessential beauty experience for my clients and needed to find a place where it would be the expectation not the exception. I was evolving from being a student, to a licensed professional to an entrepreneur.

Entrepreneurship is not for the faint at heart, but anything worth having is worth working for. I had to keep that same energy day after day, month after month and year after year. Birthing my new baby, The Pynk Butterfly brand, was part of my evolution personally and professionally. It is one thing to love doing hair, it is another thing to build a beauty brand. I had to give myself permission to push past the nay-sayers/doubters and focus on all the joy my new baby would bring to my life.

The Pynk Butterfly has been spreading its wings since 2006. From The Pynk Butterfly Hair Studio, The Pynk Butterfly Glamour Spa, The Pynk Butterfly Signature Salon & Spa, to The Pynk Butterfly Salon and now The Salon by Pynk. The evolution was never televised nor was it advertised by me. I have never given out a business card. In fact, my clients were my walking billboards. After each visit, they would leave with five business cards to hand out to people that inquired about who styled their hair. I couldn't take compliments and never wanted the attention on me, because it was never about me. It was always about the brand. A brand that over fifty beauty professionals have deposited in, as they honed their craft and elevated their careers. I find myself truly grateful for each and every one of them who have shared in the evolution of my baby, The Pynk Butterfly.

To tell the little girl in Georgia braiding her dolls' hair, the Spelmanite in the dorms doing her friends' hair or even the woman cuffed to the corporate ladder at Philip Morris USA that one day she would not only become an entrepreneur, but an award-winning master stylist, and creator and owner of a haircare product line, might have fallen on deaf ears.

There is one thing that I have learned through my evolution, is God's plan can never be stopped. Once I gave myself permission to rest in His plan for my life and be a willing participant in what He wanted to do with and through me, I found beauty in the evolution.

Permission Slip

I, _____

grant myself permission to Evolve. I am a willing and active participant in who I am becoming. I will lean into my observations and experiences to learn and embrace the beauty of evolution.

_____
Your Signature

Note To Self...

EVOLVE

The Following twelve pages have the permission slips printed individually. You are able to cut them out and keep them in plain view to remind yourself of the permissions that have been granted

Permission Slip

I, _____

grant myself permission to Change My Mind. I no longer must stick to my original plans. From new experiences and relationships, to establishing elevated goals and a fresh outlook, I am excited for what is to come.

_____
Your Signature

Permission Slip

I, _____

grant myself permission to Celebrate Me. I no longer have to wait for others to recognize my accomplishments. I will give myself a gold star and I have my own confetti to throw in the air. The party of one is the best party.

_____
Your Signature

Permission Slip

I, _____ grant myself permission to Give Myself Space. I no longer must remain attached to what and who no longer serves the person I am, and the person I am becoming. Space allows room for growth, and I am excited for what will bloom.

_____
Your Signature

Permission Slip

I, _____

grant myself permission to Protect My Peace. I accept that I cannot be everything to everybody. I am a resource used by God to be a blessing to His people. I will be mindful of how I use my resources of time, energy and money.

_____
Your Signature

Permission Slip

I, _____
grant myself permission to Stretch Myself. I will no longer confine myself to what, who or where is comfortable and familiar. I will stretch beyond the limitations I have placed on myself.

_____
Your Signature

Permission Slip

I, _____

grant myself permission to Remove My Mask. I have hidden behind fear for far too long. I will silence the thoughts and ideas that try to keep me hidden. It is time for me to step up and step out. It is time for my light to shine.

_____
Your Signature

Permission Slip

I, _____
grant myself permission to
Prioritize Myself. I am committed
to making and keeping
appointments with myself. I am
no longer preserving anyone's
feelings at the cost of my own. I
am a priority and not an option, to
myself or anyone who has the
luxury of being connected to me.

_____
Your Signature

Permission Slip

I, _____
grant myself permission to Trust God's Plan. I am no longer bound to the plans and timelines I created for my life. I will trust God's plans and rest in knowing He has already worked it out, so I do not need to try and figure it out.

_____
Your Signature

Permission Slip

I, _____

grant myself permission to Dream BIG. I will not become scared of what I see, but inspired to take the limits off and elevate my expectations. Better, greater and bigger are coming!

_____
Your Signature

Permission Slip

I, _____

grant myself permission to Lose to Win. I understand I can no longer continue to carry the emotional baggage. I have to lose the limitations I have placed on God and myself to see and understand what lies ahead positions me to win.

_____
Your Signature

Permission Slip

I, _____

grant myself permission to Pursue What I Love. I will no longer be confined to familiarity. I will take the lid off the can of possibilities and opportunities to discover and pursue what I love.

_____
Your Signature

Permission Slip

I, _____

grant myself permission to Evolve. I am a willing and active participant in who I am becoming. I will lean into my observations and experiences to learn and embrace the beauty of evolution.

_____
Your Signature

About the Author

A native of Athens, Georgia, Jessica Reese came to call South Carolina home in 1999. Upon graduating from Spelman College in Atlanta, Georgia, she accepted a position with a Fortune 5 company in Sales & Marketing, climbing the corporate ladder for 8 years. After much thought and prayer, she made the decision to step out on faith and give up what she called her "golden handcuffs" and pursue her lifelong dream of thriving in the beauty industry.

Shortly before graduating from Kenneth Shuler School of Cosmetology in 2006, The Pynk Butterfly beauty brand was birthed in the form of the first of 5 salons that were to be opened. (The Pynk Butterfly Hair Studio, The Pynk Butterfly Glamour Spa, The Pynk Butterfly Signature Salon & Spa, The Pynk Butterfly Salon, and The Salon by PYNK). With her beauty brand, Jessica has developed her own line of products, employed over 50 beauty professionals, and franchised her brand to 2 other aspiring salon owners.

Jessica's love for this industry has taken her to many places stateside and internationally such as Botswana, Johannesburg and China. From styling celebrities to being on set for photoshoots and movies, Jessica seeks to leave a mark and inspire others to, in her own words "Dare to Fly."